"Clarity, insight and personal authenticity permeate these reflections for daily life. In engaging conversation with her readers Kate Ritger describes and explores graced opportunities in the particularities of life in light of values and practices integral to the *Rule of Benedict* and Benedictine community living. This daybook is a compassionate and encouraging mirror for her readers, one in wh٠ ٠ ill see more clearly the transforming possibilitie٠ ٠ "

Katherine Howar٠
Saint Benedict's ٠

"Discover a way that the spiri ٠٠٠ ٠an come alive while growing green. Using stories, w ٠٠٠ , and personal experience, Kate Ritger gives flesh to this ancient text in a refreshing new way. Like the leaves and fruit of a plant, the Chapters of the Rule of Benedict can nourish a hunger."

Josue Behnen, OSB,
Spirituality Center
Saint Benedict's Monastery, St Joseph, MN

"Kate Ritger reminds readers of the daily process of being mindful. With a keen sense for finding the sacred in the ordinary, Ritger poses a challenge for readers to create a space for Benedictine meditation in their lives. The reflections paint a local picture on a timeless rule lived out in the 21st century and express the truthfulness of a life lived in the spirit of Saint Benedict."

Nickolas Kleespie, OSB
Saint John's Abbey, Collegeville, MN

Benedictine Living

Reflections for Prayer and Meditation

Kate Ritger

LITURGICAL PRESS

Collegeville, Minnesota

www.litpress.org

Cover design by Stefan Killen Design. Cover photo © Thinkstock.

Scripture texts in this work are taken from the *New Revised Standard Version Bible: Catholic Edition* © 1989, 1993, Division of Christian Education of the National Council of the Churches of Christ in the United States of America. Used by permission. All rights reserved.

Quotations from the Rule of St. Benedict are taken from *Rule of Saint Benedict 1980.* Edited by Timothy Fry. Collegeville, MN: Liturgical Press, 1981. Used with permission.

ISBN 978-0-8146-4907-7   ISBN 978-0-8146-3787-6 (ebook)

Contents

Moderation

Stability

Peace

Humility

Day 1

All who exalt themselves will be humbled, and those who humble themselves will be exalted.

—Luke 14:11; see Rule of Benedict 7

When you burn dinner, do you say to yourself, "I'm a failure; how could I be so stupid to walk away from the stove?" Or do you say, "Oh, what a silly mistake, let's pull out soup from the freezer instead"? When you make a flippant and biting comment to a coworker, do you say to yourself, "I'm a terrible person," or "Gosh, that just flew out of my mouth, it was a mistake"? There's a difference happening here, and the difference is between shame and guilt.

Brené Brown, a professor of social work, defines shame as "the intensely painful feeling or experience of believing we are flawed and therefore unworthy of acceptance and belonging."[1] Shame focuses on who we are at our core. Guilt, on the other hand, is the fact of having made a mistake; therefore, it focuses on our actions and how they match up with our values and beliefs.

This is what God believes about us at our core: "The word of the LORD came to me saying, 'Before I formed you in the womb I knew you'" (Jer 1:4-5). And "Like living stones, let yourselves be built into a spiritual house . . . 'See, I am laying in Zion a stone, a cornerstone chosen and precious; and whoever believes in him will not be put to shame'" (1 Pet 2:5-6). We are God's beloved children. God does not look at us with shame. God does not compare us to other people. God does not expect us to be perfect. God does not need to exaggerate our gifts and abilities. Throughout the Rule, Benedict, so steeped in Scripture, gives countless opportunities to try again when we've made a mistake.

> How do you respond when you've done something you wish you hadn't?
>
> How does Brown's articulation of shame and guilt resonate with your life?

Take a moment today to remember you are God's beloved.

Note

1. Brené Brown, *I Thought It Was Just Me* (New York: Penguin, 2007), 5.

Humility

Day 2

All who exalt themselves will be humbled, and those who humble themselves will be exalted.

—Luke 14:11; see Rule of Benedict 7

Since 1939, thousands of people around the world have been engaging the spiritual program of Alcoholics Anonymous and working the twelve steps. The first of the steps helps people to acknowledge their lack of power over alcohol and their inability to manage their lives. Alcoholism is a disease; like cancer or diabetes it cannot be cured or overcome through willpower, and it is not a decision to be an alcoholic.

Someone in the program said to me that to practice this first step is to admit on a daily basis that there is emptiness in our lives. Emptiness is not in and of itself a bad thing. She reflected that emptiness can be turned into spaciousness if we invite God to be part of it.

There are seventy-three chapters in the Rule of Benedict and humility ranks number seven. The first step of humility, as Benedict writes it, is that one "keeps the fear of God always before [one's] eyes (Ps 35[36]:2) and never forgets it" (RB 7.10). Joan Chittister, OSB, comments, "When we make ourselves God, no one in the world is safe in our presence. Humility, in other words, is the basis for right relationships in life."[1]

Right relationship with God, ourselves, and anyone else in our lives demands spiritual fitness. Are we talking to God? Are we going to God with other people? And are we doing it frequently and consistently? These grounding questions can bring us into the spaciousness of God's love.

Name and describe someone you know who invites God to transform his or her emptiness into spaciousness. What does this look like?

What are things you would like to do, but don't? What stands in your way?

Take a moment today to lovingly admit your emptiness.

Note

1. Joan Chittister, *The Rule of Benedict: Insights for the Ages* (New York: Crossroad, 1992), 62.

Humility

Day 3

All who exalt themselves will be humbled, and those who humble themselves will be exalted.

—Luke 14:11; see Rule of Benedict 7

Annually I go through a hiring process for summer and fall garden assistants. I often find that the college students are hesitant to talk about what would make them a good fit for the job. Perhaps this is an example of what Marianne Williamson describes in her famous quotation from *A Return to Love*: "Our deepest fear is not that we are inadequate. Our deepest fear is that we are powerful beyond measure. It is our light, not our darkness that most frightens us. We ask ourselves, Who am I to be brilliant, gorgeous, talented, fabulous? Actually, who are you *not* to be? You are a child of God."[1]

The Rule of Benedict's fourth and fifth steps in humility are perseverance and self-revelation. Life in community can be about the almost constant experience of brushing up against each other and recognizing our abilities and limitations. And just like anywhere else, life in community can be a place to hide from ourselves and others.

"[Jesus] said to them, 'Is a lamp brought in to be put under the bushel basket, or under the bed, and not on the lampstand? For there is nothing hidden, except to be disclosed; nor is anything secret, except to come to light. Let anyone with ears to hear listen!'" (Mark 4:21-23). In this passage Jesus commands there to be no secrets, virtues self-consciously hidden or vices tucked away in shame. Benedictines will persevere in this life together through honest and kind self-revelation.

> Who are you afraid to be, both in strength and in weakness?
>
> Who invites you to growthful self-revelation?

Take a moment today to reflect on your light.

Note

1. Marianne Williamson, *A Return to Love* (New York: HarperCollins, 1992), 165.

Humility

Day 4

All who exalt themselves will be humbled, and those who humble themselves will be exalted.

—Luke 14:11; see Rule of Benedict 7

Benedict's eighth, ninth, tenth, and eleventh steps of humility invite us to participate in a community of learners who are nothing alone. Joan Chittister notes, "When we know our place in the universe, we can afford to value the place of others. We need them, in fact, to make up what is wanting in us."[1]

Parker Palmer, Quaker educator and spiritual writer, tells a story about visiting a university to give lectures. Before arriving, Palmer told the host professor that he would speak for about twenty minutes and then open the rest of the hour and a half time slot to conversation. The professor said it wouldn't work; the students wouldn't talk. Palmer did it anyway. At first it was horrible; no one talked and he felt like he was drowning. Then a small hand went up in the back of the room and someone responded. The comment wasn't brilliant but it was a start; the person took a risk, and soon more students followed and an excellent conversation ensued.

Palmer describes education as a group of people gathered around a body of material—for example, a poem, a story, or a theory—responding to "What do you know about this?" Often, as the professor anticipated, people are resistant and sometimes respond in frustration to this educational process. "Shouldn't the teacher provide the wisdom?" "I don't want to hear from my classmates and I'm certainly not paying money to hear myself talk." We all have something to give, but we may not know it yet.

After the class ended, the professor walked Palmer out of the building and said, "You used the most amazing technique; I've never seen it before!" "Oh?" Palmer responded, "What was that?" "When a student was about to respond you waved them on and said 'Please.' And after they finished you said 'Thank you.'" Palmer said, "I was drowning up there! Of course I said 'please' and 'thank you'!"

Sometimes it is horrifying to recognize our vulnerability and need for others. At other times it is an immense relief to know and release ourselves into our interconnectedness. We are at the same time needy and desperately thankful for the role of others in our lives. Over and over again Benedict reminds us that we are beginners on a spiritual journey to God together.[2]

> When are you humble? In what circumstances is it difficult for you to be humble? Explain.
>
> When are you filled with gratitude? In what circumstances is it difficult for you to be grateful? Explain.

Take a moment today to interact with someone in a way that honors his or her place in your life.

Notes

1. Joan Chittister, *The Rule of Benedict: Insights for the Ages* (New York: Crossroad, 1992), 72.

2. Rule of Benedict Prol. 2, 4, 5, 73.

Stewardship

Day 1

Creation is the Lord's and we are its keepers.

—Upon This Tradition[1]

My sister used to have a T-shirt from Muir Woods in California that read, "I am a keeper of the trees." I imagine Dr. Seuss's fluffy yellow Lorax popping out of a crevice in a giant redwood tree to claim the same statement. Some translations of the book of Genesis also use this language of keeping: "The LORD God took the man and put him in the garden of Eden to till it and keep it" (Gen 2:15). And the American Confederation of Benedictine Sisters similarly defines stewardship around keeping: "that we use what we are and what we have for the transformation of culture because creation is the Lord's and we are its keepers; we hold it in trust."[2]

How often do I think of myself as a "keeper"? To "keep" has a completely different tone than to "have dominion over" or even to "care for." "To keep" suggests a radically different type of relationship. If I'm going to keep my three-year-old niece's secret,

I'm going to savor the special relationship we have, and hold her secret safely until she wants it to be shared with the rest of the family. We've made a covenant in love. Famously, God said to Noah, "This is the sign of the covenant that I make between me and you and every living creature that is with you, for all future generations: I have set my bow in the clouds, and it shall be a sign of the covenant between me and the earth" (Gen 9:12-13).

Recycle, conserve water, turn off lights and appliances when not in use, carpool, grow your own food, bring canvas bags to the store, combine errands into one trip to save fuel—all of these tips could appear in a handout on living on a budget, but they are also responses to being a keeper. The sisters of Saint Benedict in St. Joseph, Minnesota, are also keepers of shared goods: shared cars, an internal swap shop, vegetable and flower gardens, financial resources, a library, a fitness space, yard care equipment . . . and the list goes on.

> For what/whom are you a good caretaker or keeper? In what ways?
>
> For what/whom are you not a good caretaker or keeper?

Take a moment today to reflect on your covenant relationship with God.

Notes

1. Conference of American Benedictine Prioresses, *Upon This Tradition III: Of All Good Gifts: A Statement on the Nature of Stewardship in the Lives of American Benedictine Sisters*, ed. Ruth Fox, OSB (St. Joseph, MN: 1980), http://www.msb.net/Community_About_UTT_UTT3.html.
2. Ibid.

Stewardship

Day 2

Regard all utensils and goods of the monastery as sacred vessels of the altar.

—Rule of Benedict 31.10

One Sunday during the distribution of Communion at Saint Benedict's Monastery, a wine carafe was broken in the hands of a young woman in early formation with the community. The schola was leading the communion hymn and while the soft "tink" of breaking glass was hardly noticeable, small shards and several big pieces covered the altar cloth. I assume that the young woman was horrified, her face washed in red. She tried to maintain her composure and gather the pieces, but another sacristan came to her rescue, and I'm guessing told her to leave it for the time being and clean it up after the liturgy. A sacred vessel of the altar was broken.

There are at least two ways of reading "regard all utensils and goods of the monastery as sacred vessels of the altar"; both are insightful. One way is to regard all utensils as if they are as holy as the sacred vessels of the altar: clean your garden rake as gingerly as you wash a communion cup, tidy your car as thoroughly as you clean the chapel's sanctuary, and maintain the dishwasher as meticulously as you service the organ.

A second way of reading this line is to hold the sacred vessels of the altar with the holiness we hold all "ordinary" utensils of our lives. The eucharistic dishes, the presider's garments, the Sacramentary, and the wine carafe are all part of life; they can be broken, ripped, or torn, and we aren't meant to be attached to them. I think this second line of thinking offered compassion to the novice on that Sunday morning.

What are the ordinary and sacred vessels of your life?

How do you interact with these vessels?

Take a moment today to give thanks for the vessels of your life.

Stewardship

Day 3

Whenever new clothing is received, the old should be returned at once and stored in a wardrobe for the poor.

—Rule of Benedict 55.9

I wish Benedict would have written "stored in a wardrobe for those who need it" instead of "for the poor," but maybe the distinction wasn't important in his context. It's important in my context as I work for food justice in central Minnesota. There are many reasons why people don't have or eat fresh, local food. Cost, location, and time are three big reasons. We are all in need in different ways, and it is through personal relationships and sharing our wealth that our needs are met.

Joan Chittister reflects that "Benedictine spirituality does not understand a world that is full of gorgeous garbage while [others] lack the basics of life."[1] At Common Ground Garden of Saint Benedict's Monastery, we grow and distribute food. Distributing food is complicated work. Each week produce is harvested and distributed to garden subscribers, folks in the area who pay a lump sum in the spring for fresh vegetables throughout the growing season. On Fridays we sell to the St. Joseph Farmers' Market patrons. We sell wholesale to the Minnesota Street Market, the local food and art co-op in St. Joseph, and Nick's Third Floor, a local food restaurant in downtown St. Cloud. Friends and community members who contribute to the garden in a variety of ways receive vegetables. We also regularly take produce to the St. Joseph Community Food Shelf and the St. Cloud Catholic Charities Food Shelf. Last, the sisters of Saint Benedict's Monastery and the gardeners eat a lot of produce. Hundreds of people eat of this one garden and make the effort possible.

In what ways are you wealthy/blessed? What and how do you share?

Make a "gratitude list." For example, include specific physical resources, people, and communities that enrich your life.

Take a moment today to learn about the path of an item in your life that is "thrown away." For example, clothes not purchased from a department store, food pulled from grocery store shelves, new cars that are not sold from the lot.

Note

1. Joan Chittister, *The Rule of Benedict: Insights for the Ages* (New York: Crossroad, 1992), 146.

Prayer

Day 1

The function of prayer is to change my own mind, to put on the mind of Christ, to enable grace to break into me.

—Joan Chittister, *Wisdom Distilled from the Daily*[1]

"It seems like cedar waxwings are everywhere! . . . God shows me love through their presence." This is how a friend recently described a shift she experienced in her prayer life. She's an oblate of the Sisters of Saint Benedict, a graduate of their college, and recently moved to the east coast with her husband. My friend misses proximity to the monastery for prayer, spiritual direction, and relationships with the sisters, and was aching to deepen her faith life when she met another oblate who lives in the area and who started a "school of Christian spirituality." A number of Christian churches have partnered together to offer classes on spirituality and prayer. My friend started taking the classes, met other people who want to grow in their faith, and found herself recognizing God's presence in unexpected places.

My friend commented, "The cedar waxwings have been special birds to me for a long time. Every day this week I saw them, flying out of the tall oak to the berry bush in our backyard, and then back again. And then this morning we saw them as we walked to church. I have wanted to grow closer to God, and through the birds, God is showing me love." No place is an unexpected place for God. God is with us as we get cut off in traffic. God is with us in difficult conversations with partners and coworkers. God is with us as we find our way in new places and in new communities. God is with us. As Joan Chittister writes, "prayer is designed to enable people to realize that God is in the world around them."[2]

> Name and reflect on an experience you've had of prayer opening you to a new way of being, seeing, doing, or responding. Describe this experience.
>
> Describe an experience of seeing God's love for you in an "unexpected place."

Take a moment today to receive singing birds as God's invitation to come closer.

Notes

1. Joan Chittister, OSB, *Wisdom Distilled from the Daily: Living the Rule of St. Benedict Today* (San Francisco: HarperCollins, 1990), 35.
2. Ibid., 28.

Prayer

Day 2

The function of prayer is to change my own mind, to put on the mind of Christ, to enable grace to break into me.

—Joan Chittister, *Wisdom Distilled from the Daily*[1]

Online dating forced me to remember I am beloved.
When I signed up for an online dating service, I knew it was going to take time and energy. I wanted to fully engage the process—I was serious about seeking a life partner. What I didn't anticipate was the vulnerability I would feel. You write a bit about your life, what brings you joy, what you hope for in a partner, and post a few photos of yourself—click submit and you're out there for all to see.

I opened my email the day after I signed up and saw that no one had contacted me. A week went by and no one wrote. I wrote friendly little emails to men who were interesting and attractive to me. No one responded. "Why doesn't anyone like me? Is my description of myself too serious? Aren't my pictures flattering? Do I live too far away?"

These are not questions that helped me to love myself. These questions perpetuated the idea that something was wrong with me and I was not worthy of another person's love. If a man did not write to me it was because we were not a match, and that was not my fault, nor was it something I wanted to change. I quickly realized that if I was going to make it through my six-month subscription to the service, I needed to wholeheartedly believe that I am lovable in God's sight, my sight, and the sight of others. It is one of the best prayer lessons of my life.

When is it easy/difficult for you to know God's love?

Describe a prayerful person you know.

Take a moment today to speak kindly to yourself of your self-worth.

Note

1. Joan Chittister, OSB, *Wisdom Distilled from the Daily: Living the Rule of St. Benedict Today* (San Francisco: HarperCollins, 1990), 35.

Prayer

Day 3

The function of prayer is to change my own mind, to put on the mind of Christ, to enable grace to break into me.

—Joan Chittister, *Wisdom Distilled from the Daily*[1]

One day during my oblate live-in experience, a sister at the lunch table commented, "You know, sometimes I kind of zone out during Liturgy of the Hours and the psalms just roll over me and don't connect to my life much. But other times I'm so aware that even if the psalms aren't voicing *my* experience at the moment, I am voicing the experience of someone somewhere." Somewhere in the world a person is wailing a lament. Somewhere a person is raising a joyful voice. Prayer reminds us that the earth does not revolve around us, but that we are part of the experience of the universe, and that our prayer can offer compassion and support to someone who needs it.

I physically feel different when I remember my presence and prayer in the world stretches beyond my everyday life. My shoulders relax and stretch down my back. It feels like my heart, my entire chest cavity, opens up and out toward the world around me. While I expand my scope of compassion, I also receive a bigger range of compassion.

> How do you pray?
>
> How do you live prayerfully, with attention to God and those around you?

Take a moment today to pray for someone you don't know.

Note

1. Joan Chittister, OSB, *Wisdom Distilled from the Daily: Living the Rule of St. Benedict Today* (San Francisco: HarperCollins, 1990), 35.

Obedience

Day 1

Obedience, Benedict says—the willingness to listen for the voice of God in life.

—Joan Chittister, OSB, *The Rule of Benedict*[1]

The gospel reading from John about "doubting Thomas" recently prompted new reflections for me (John 20:19-31). Spiritual writer Kathy Hendricks comments in *Give Us This Day*, "like so many others, I tend more towards cynicism and suspicion over news that sounds too good to be true . . . we expect the worst from our leaders, our media, our celebrities, and, at times, even our families."[2]

Before reading Hendricks's reflection, I wouldn't have named myself a cynical person, but I too find myself casually saying, "it is yet to be seen" or "we'll see if they show up." With these statements I think I am protecting myself from being constantly disappointed or identified as naively optimistic. I believe that God wants a life for me that overflows with joy, love, and goodness. Other people disappoint me and add to my cynicism and suspicion, but Hendricks leaves someone important off the list: me. I often disappoint myself with my blunderings and self-centered slipups, and when I let my fears get in the way of who I really want to be.

Obedience in the monastic tradition continually wraps us in wisdom that transforms our brokenness to wholeness, and calls us to draw closer to God. Obedience in this case calls me to self-compassion. "Do not fear, for I am with you" (Isa 41:10), and "stand and walk, and sin no more" (see Matt 9:5). I deserve it. And as Jesus said to Thomas, he too says to me, "Peace be with you. . . . Put your finger here and see my hands. Reach out your hand and put it in my side. Do not doubt but believe" (John 20:26-27).

> What cynicisms and suspicions get in your way of listening for the voice of God?
>
> Who calls you back to obedience?

Take a moment today to offer yourself compassion.

Notes

1. Joan Chittister, *The Rule of Benedict: Insights for the Ages* (New York: Crossroad, 1992), 20.

2. Kathy Hendricks, "Skeptics," Reflection, *Give Us This Day* 3, no. 4 (April 2013): 74.

Obedience

Day 2

Obedience, Benedict says—the willingness to listen for the voice of God in life.

—Joan Chittister, OSB, *The Rule of Benedict*[1]

My basketball career didn't extend beyond grade school, but I learned an important spiritual lesson in it: pivot to new options. If I am dribbling down the court and stop, I cannot resume dribbling, but I can pivot, hold one foot in place and rotate around to take a shot at the basket or find a teammate open to receive a pass. Obedience meets us at the pivot point.

If I'm going about my day and something happens that throws me off course, I am brought to a pivot point. Maybe I forgot my wallet at home so I don't have money to stop at the grocery store. Maybe a coworker said something that touched a sore spot in me of embarrassment. Maybe I received a bill that I wasn't expecting. Regardless of the situational or systemic episode, I have the opportunity to pivot to new options.

Joan Chittister reminds us in *Wisdom Distilled from the Daily*, "No one really has full control of their own lives. . . . Conversion . . . is a willingness to let go, to be led beyond where we are, to where we can be."[2] Saint Benedict says that obedience is listening for the voice of God in life. What option can I pivot toward that opens me to new life? How can I live into my strength and freedom? How can I lean on God and other loving people in my life more? How can I be a prophet of justice? Obedience to God's will calls us to pivot from death to new life.

> What practices do you have for opening yourself to daily conversion, to be willing to be led beyond where you are now?

Take a moment today to identify options you have in response to a "stopping point."

Notes

1. Joan Chittister, *The Rule of Benedict: Insights for the Ages* (New York: Crossroad, 1992), 20.

2. Joan Chittister, OSB, *Wisdom Distilled from the Daily: Living the Rule of St. Benedict Today* (San Francisco: HarperCollins, 1990), 134, 144.

Obedience

Day 3

Obedience is a blessing to be shown by all.

—Rule of Benedict 71.1

More often than I'd like to admit, I steer clear of publications that I perceive are written from the other side of the ideological spectrum. And I rarely invite people to dinner who annoy me, don't fit in my social circles, or live in ways I deem irresponsible.

Obviously this isn't the model Jesus gave us. Jesus healed lepers and cripples, ate with tax collectors and prostitutes, and graciously received the anointing of women. Saint Benedict also pushes our comfort zones to include people we might not initially think are part of our community. It isn't until chapter 58 of the Rule that Benedict even discusses how the monastery should receive members, implying that it isn't the first thing on his mind, and in that chapter there is no evidence that admittance is based on being rich or poor, liberal or conservative, or fashionable or frumpy.

In chapter 61 on the reception of visiting monastics Benedict writes, "A visiting [monastic] from far away will perhaps present [oneself] and wish to stay as a guest in the monastery." He or she "may, indeed, with all humility and love make some reasonable criticisms or observations, which the abbot [or prioress] should prudently consider; it is possible that the Lord guided him [or her] to the monastery for this very purpose" (1, 4). Not only are people from other groups allowed to live in the monastery but they are also welcomed as a possible gift from God, with an ear to learn from them. Benedict constantly calls us to broaden our perception of who can be instruments of God's grace.

> Who would you not invite to a dinner party? Why?
>
> Who could you easily receive criticism from? Why?

Take a moment today to read something you would typically pass off as "too liberal" or "too conservative."

Community Living

Day 1

Kindness shown them.

—See Rule of Benedict 34.4

Elie Wiesel wrote, "What God gave Adam was not forgiveness from sin; what God gave Adam was the chance to begin again."[1] Hurts, misunderstandings, conflicts, and differences in opinion are natural and normal parts of all relationships and community living. So also is the practice of reconciling, or re-circling. To re-circle is to come around again to the hurts and joys, pains and moments of gratitude in a relationship. All of it, our vulnerabilities and giftedness, are part and parcel of who we are and cannot be separated or left behind in our relationships.

And as we come around again, we need to bring a heart of compassion, starting with self-compassion. Paul Gilbert, in his book *The Compassionate Mind*, identifies eight reasons why we resist self-compassion: (1) we have been taught to put others before ourselves, (2) we think we are already self-compassionate, (3) we think it is weak or soft to be self-compassionate, (4) we think we don't deserve it, (5) we fear becoming proud, (6) we dislike ourselves, (7) self-compassion raises buried issues, and (8) we believe self-compassion might prevent us from the hard work of growing.[2]

My experience has repeatedly been that relationships, specifically community living, either bring me to a breaking point where self-compassion or implosion are the only options left, or members of my community show me that the light of compassion I endlessly shine on others needs to include me. My resistance to self-compassion is deep, but thankfully it is rising to the surface more and more and I am able to consciously choose a different response. And as a result, I experience a dance between the kindness I show myself, kindness others offer me, and re-circling in my relationships with myself, God, and people in my community.

What have you found to be helpful as you "re-circle" in your relationships?

Why do you resist self-compassion? Which of Gilbert's reasons resonates with you?

Take a moment today to invite greater self-compassion into your life.

Notes

1. Quoted in Joan Chittister, *The Rule of Benedict: Insights for the Ages* (New York: Crossroad, 1992), 159.

2. Paul Gilbert, *The Compassionate Mind: A New Approach to Life's Challenges* (Oakland, CA: New Harbinger, 2010).

Community Living

Day 2

It was distributed to each as any had need.

—Acts 4:35; see Rule of Benedict 34

I saw a family at church with a teenage son, a grade-school-age daughter, and a younger son with Down's syndrome. It was obvious to me that the child with Down's was a special part of the family: the sister held his hand as they entered church and helped him dip his hand into the baptismal font and sign himself with the sign of the cross. As they settled into their pew, the older boy happily pulled his little brother onto his lap and whispered gently in his ear. After Mass, I noticed the family again, and as they headed toward the door, I overheard the girl complain, "It's not fair, I want to go to the beach. Why does he always need to take a nap after lunch?" The dad swept up his daughter into his arms and reminded her about how her brother gets tired faster than she does, and they would go to the beach after his nap. The little boy had a need and the family structured its plans around it.

Chapter 34 in the Rule, citing Acts 4:35, says nothing about distributing goods based on who worked the hardest, who was the favorite, who was the most charismatic, or who looked the part. It says, "Whoever needs less should thank God and not be distressed, but whoever needs more should feel humble because of his [or her] weakness, not self-important because of the kindness shown him [or her]. In this way all the members will be at peace" (3-5). If someone's body is constantly cold, perhaps he needs an extra sweater or set of warm socks. If a member of the monastery works outside the community at a site not convenient for public transportation, she probably needs a car at her regular disposal. If a family member is studying to complete a degree, he likely needs more time to devote to reading than his usual household chores.

It's easy to admit that as children we complained of unfairness, but we also complain as adults. As Benedict notes, peace comes when we are not distressed that our "little brother" received something we did not need, and he is not gloating over his "extra helping." Both perspectives draw us into more intimate community that leans together for support, not apart in competition.

How do you respond when life doesn't feel fair?

When is it easy/difficult for you to receive out of your need?

Take a moment today to name what is distributed to you based on your need.

Community Living

Day 3

Everything they owned was held in common.

—Acts 4:32; see Rule of Benedict 33

Brother David Steindl-Rast, OSB, writes, "Community is always posed between two poles: solitude and togetherness . . . they make each other possible."[1] Many people are familiar with the introvert/extrovert distinction: introverts generally need time alone to be recharged, and extroverts generally get energy from being with a group. Personally, I fall close to the center of the spectrum, but definitely on the introvert side: I love being with people but if I don't have an evening or two a week alone, I get frazzled and crabby. Benedict was attentive to this dynamic.

Brother David goes on to say, "Without togetherness community disperses; without solitude community collapses into a mass, a crowd."[2] People need to come together around something, a common mission (for example, raising money for a new town park), a shared hobby (knitting or softball), or a mutual experience (having grade-school-age children), otherwise they are just folks uninterested in anything beyond their independent lives. Similarly, if people don't have a sense of who they are, fed by knowledge of self in solitude, they are just a crowd of people.

Parker Palmer comes at this in *A Hidden Wholeness* in another way: "To understand true self—which knows *who* we are in our inwardness and *whose* we are in the larger world—we need both the interior intimacy that comes with solitude and the otherness that comes with community."[3] *Who* and *whose*, solitude and community—they enliven each other and ground us for community life.

> "Whose" are you?
>
> How do solitude and being with others support your coming to know "whose" you are and how you live as a result?

Take a moment today to think about how you balance solitude and community in your daily rhythms.

Notes

1. David Steindl-Rast, OSB, "Contemplative Community," *Benedictines*, vol. xxvi, no. 2 (Summer 1971).

2. Ibid.

3. Parker Palmer, *A Hidden Wholeness: The Journey toward an Undivided Life* (San Francisco: Jossey-Bass, 2004), 54.

Authority

Day 1

Advice from [one] who loves you.

—Rule of Benedict Prol. 1

Yuck, two words I don't like, let alone together: authority and advice. I have to work pretty hard when I hear "authority" not to bristle and worry about who is trying to lord power over me. And I think it's my training in spiritual companioning that prompts cringes from the idea of someone giving me advice, as if I'm not smart enough or in tune enough with my own wisdom to know how to live. Slow down a minute, and don't overlook the end of the statement: "loves you."

Benedict is not instructing me to submit to just anyone; Benedict is instructing me to submit to someone who loves me. Can I trust that someone loves and honors me, and has some guidance that is of value to me? Yes, of course. I have been blessed with many wisdom figures that fit that description. And I even *seek* their guidance on a regular basis. These loving authorities know me deeply, listen with love, support my inner power, and sincerely want what is best for me. And Benedict goes on to say, an authority should "love as [is] best for each individual" (RB 64.14). I'm not just another wayward young woman when I come to my wisdom figures in distress; I am a whole person with a particular story, and they invite me to love myself more deeply through Christ.

Describe an experience you've had of authority rooted in love.

When is it easy/difficult for you to act out your authority with love? Explain.

Take a moment today to thank a loving authority in your life.

Authority

Day 2

Advice from [one] who loves you.

—Rule of Benedict Prol. 1

I lived in the monastery for six weeks several years ago as part of the Oblates in Residence program at Saint Benedict's Monastery. One evening after dinner, the sisters in my living group and I were gathered in the common living room. A few of us were playing cards and another sister sat next to a lamp reading a novel. We were all aware that 7:00 Evening Prayer was approaching. Without fuss or fanfare a sister excused herself from the table, retrieved her coat from the closet, and headed out the door and over to the oratory. Another sister did the same. Still another headed upstairs to use the restroom. No one said in a bossy way, "It's 6:54; time for all of us to go to prayer." The women respected each other's personal needs, and they responded with love for their community commitment to prayer.

Also, I didn't often see coats left in the dining room or coffee cups forgotten in the community rooms. There are coat closets, and racks by the industrial dishwasher for cups that didn't make it in the mealtime wash. And there are teams: the breakfast cooks, teams of two sisters who make hot cereal and hard/soft-boiled eggs on a rotating basis, and the dishwashing teams, sisters who wash the dishes and sanitize the dining tables. There's a sign in the dining room that no one other than the sisters pays attention to, denoting who is on dishwashing duty that week. And sisters have "charges": to clean one of the many community or public bathrooms on a weekly basis, or to tend the lawn under a honey locust tree where pods regularly fall to the ground. Many hands share the work of keeping so many community spaces clean and well tended. In Benedictine communities authority is not an end in itself. Authority is not meant to oppress people. Authority is meant to help meet people's needs. Authority is rooted in love and respect for the unique fullness of each person.

How do you exercise your authority on a daily basis?

How would you like to exercise your authority on a daily basis?

Take a moment today to do something someone else needs.

Authority

Day 3

[Deans of the monastery] are to be chosen for virtuous living and wise teaching, not for their rank.

—Rule of Benedict 21.4

The Rule of Benedict makes it clear that the prioress or abbot is a person who loves the community and acts out of love toward each individual's needs. Benedict continues to turn our modern understanding of authority on its head with details about deans in the monastery. First, if a community is rather large, deans should be chosen. The prioress/abbot is always to be focused on the needs of the community so they can live the God-life, and that potentially means inviting others to be part of the role.

Second, deans are to be people who can "share the burdens" of prioress/abbot (RB 21.3). This isn't a model of delegation that spins into micromanagement or languishes in a hands-off-until-you've-failed philosophy. Sharing the burden is rooted in common decisions, common wisdom, and common commitment.

And third, deans are to be chosen, not based on their years in community or letters after their name, but for their "virtuous living and wise teaching." Joan Chittister reminds us that "Benedictine spirituality uses authority to weld a group, not to fracture it."[1] Communities are vibrant when their hearts shine with a common dream. Deans are to be instruments of common support and teaching, not leaders of fraction groups or rivals to the prioress/abbot.

> Where do you see examples of this type of authority in your daily life (in your family, work, local community, national or international news)?
>
> What would your family, work, local community, or the national/international landscape look like if this type of authority were integrated?

Take a moment today to thank a "dean" in your life.

Note

1. Joan Chittister, *The Rule of Benedict: Insights for the Ages* (New York: Crossroad, 1992), 92.

Work

Day 1

They live by the labor of their hands.

—Rule of Benedict 48.8

Apparently Benjamin Franklin gets credit for the line "If you want something done, ask a busy person." The point being that a busy person is efficient, and good at managing her time and the innumerable items on her "to-do" list. I like my "to-do" lists and I like checking items off my "to-do" list. But more often than I'd like, I get to the end of the day, end of the month, or end of the year and feel frustrated by my busyness. I have put too much merit in the "check-off" and the accolades and recognition it has brought to me, and not as much in being present to myself, God, or others in the process of the work.

Yes, there is a lot of important work to do in the world. People need to be fed, clothed, and sheltered. Children need to learn and be entrusted with the future. Peace needs to be cultivated in every corner of the planet. And while Benedict wrote that his community was to "live by the labor of their hands," he also institutionalized breaks and drew attention to God's presence in every activity of our day. In case you weren't paying attention to God while you were working, Benedict says, "take a break, pray with your community for a bit, and take God with you to the next item on your 'to-do' list."

Where is God in your work?

Who are you outside of your work?

Take a moment today to invite God into your work.

Work

Day 2

They live by the labor of their hands.

—Rule of Benedict 48.8

I often say that "gardening is a team sport." A garden of more than three acres needs more than one gardener because of its size, but also because there are some jobs that require more than two hands at one time. For example, one person cannot carry the sixteen-foot-long "hog panels" we use to trellis our cucumbers. And, while I suppose one person could harvest one hundred watermelons—averaging ten pounds each—and move them from the field to the barn, no one would want to. The work is not only more possible but also more joyful, by working together with a team of people who bring unique skills and passions together.

A sister from Saint Benedict's Monastery shared parallel feelings about her sense of being part of her sisters' ministries. "I spend my day at the Spirituality Center and work on behalf of the community there. I'm also so proud to be part of the work of my sisters: teaching in the college, working in the parishes, writing music and texts for worship, visiting patients in the hospital, leading people into the future—I'm part of all of that too."

Another friend reminded me that when one community member's skills aren't utilized, it is a loss for everyone. When the economically "poor" among us are solely treated like people who need things given to them, the entire community misses what the "poor" have to share. Saint Paul reminds us "there are varieties of gifts, but the same Spirit; and there are varieties of services, but the same Lord . . . To each is given the manifestation of the Spirit for the common good" (1 Cor 12:4-5, 7). Together people live by the work of their hands.

When is it easy/difficult for you to be a team member?

Whose work are you thankful for?

Take a moment today to recognize the gifts of those on the margins.

Work

Day 3

So that in all things God may be glorified.

—1 Peter 4:11; see Rule of Benedict 57.9

I sing with the monastery schola and right after we've rehearsed our music, but before we head to the chapel for Sunday Eucharist, the director says, "That in all things" and we reply, "God may be glorified."

It's easy to see the work of singing in a choir as glorifying God. But are all the things I do throughout my week glorifying to God? When I think about my work in the garden, some of it certainly is: pulling bright red radishes and deep orange carrots from the ground, distributing beautiful bunches of kale and flats of juicy, sweet tomatoes, and thinking of the people, young and old, who eat and feel part of a community because of this garden. But other garden work is less obviously glorifying: shoveling and hauling wheelbarrows of compost, squatting to plant a bed with tiny rutabaga seeds, and doing just about anything while gnats circle around our heads. These tasks are sneaky in their glorifying qualities. Sometimes they feel monotonous. Sometimes they stretch muscles I'd rather not remember, and sometimes they are just annoying. But even as they annoy me and make me ache, these tasks also draw me closer to God.

The phrase "that in all things God may be glorified" helps me remember that *all* that I do, however seemingly mundane or lowly, can be a means to give glory to God. Hand weeding fragile onion seedlings is dignifying work. Spreading chicken manure around rhubarb plants that will strengthen the plants and eventually produce thick stalks is dignifying work. The phrase also pulls me out of myself to recognize that the glory and honor of anything I do comes from and returns to God. In this, I can participate in God's gracious life of love.

> What does "that in all things God may be glorified" mean to you?
>
> Describe a mundane task of your life that glorifies God.

Take a moment today to say "that in all things God may be glorified" before you begin a task.

Listening

Day 1

Listen . . . with the ear of your heart.

—Rule of Benedict Prol. 1

The woods are silent and still in the winter. Without wind, I hear only the crunch of my boots beneath me and my exhales of the cold air, and even those sounds are muffled through my thick hat. Pines are heavily laden with snow. One lean cedar is bowed over by the weight. It silently holds its posture, almost to breaking point.

As spring inches forward there are new sounds every day. Icicles drip onto sidewalks. Chickadees and robins call and sing. Snow chunks drop off car bumpers with a slushy plop. On the same walk in the woods my boots slosh and suck over the wet ground. Woodpeckers tap and drill into thawing trees.

On a drizzly summer day the rain falls from thousands of leaves to the wood's floor. Water is heard slurping into the ground of thirsty gardens and fields. The world is alive with sounds and movement: squirrels and birds talking and moving from tree to tree, crickets and grasshoppers munching and jumping, and people out for walks, laughing and talking, playing Frisbee and swinging in hammocks.

Dry autumn leaves rattle on the branches. My shoes crunch as if I'm walking over a path of tortilla chips. Bonfires crackle and spit, mice scurry and squeak, and thousands of geese honk as they fly overhead.

> When and where is it easy for you to listen?
>
> When and where is it difficult for you to listen?

Take a moment today to go for a walk and describe what you see and hear.

Listening

Day 2

Listen . . . with the ear of your heart.

—Rule of Benedict Prol. 1

Lectio divina is a monastic prayer form that literally means "sacred reading." *Lectio* is repetitive. A sacred text, most often a passage from the Bible, is read out loud at a deliberate pace several times. Between each reading there are pauses for silence and reflection on how the passage speaks to the reader's life. The reader is also invited to listen for a call to do or be in a new way, a way that shares God's love in the world.

Prayer, like anything we do on a regular basis, shapes who we are and how we experience and make sense of the world. For years I have started my morning with about fifteen minutes of stretching and yoga, and since I started gardening full-time that has expanded to about thirty minutes every morning and periodically in the evening as well. Even during my garden "off-season" I automatically wake up and roll out of bed onto my yoga mat. The movements slowly bring me out of sleep, wake up my muscles, lengthen my spine, kick-start my circulation and digestion systems, and honor the gift of my unique body.

The same is true of eating habits. Over the course of decades my grandma weaned my grandpa off sugary desserts. She cut recipes' sugar allotment bit by bit and then one day at a church dinner my grandpa commented about the excessive sweetness of someone else's homemade dessert. These habits are undeniably healthy, but they aren't always easy, fun, or pain-free.

From my experience with Benedictines, *lectio* is a meaningful prayer form, a healthy habit in their day, and an integrated way of listening. Sometimes we hear things that are joyful, healing, and transformative. And sometimes we hear things that are upsetting, embarrassing, and convicting. As Joan Chittister reminds us, "listen with compassion . . . listen for the truth of a thing . . . [and] obey what makes your heart more human."[1]

How are you being called to habits of healthful listening?

Describe an experience in your life that has made "your heart more human."

Take a moment today to listen with the ear of your heart.

Note

1. Joan Chittister, OSB, *Wisdom Distilled from the Daily: Living the Rule of St. Benedict Today* (San Francisco: HarperCollins, 1990), 145–46.

Listening

Day 3

Listen . . . with the ear of your heart.

—Rule of Benedict Prol. 1

Listening seems so simple, but it is a fine art and there are often so many challenges to listening well. Sometimes, the things we need to hear are drowned out by competing noises: Could I hear my Mom over the noise of traffic? Did I hear the directions to the restaurant clearly? Sometimes, we are too distracted to really listen: Was I coming up with a solution to her problem instead of just listening to it? Did all the other things on my mind prevent me from listening to his body language as he shared about his struggle at work? And sometimes we don't listen to the important things: Did I hear and respect his need for space? Did I hear the weariness of my own heart?

"Listen with the ear of your heart" suggests conscientious listening. It suggests that we listen with our whole selves, including the abilities and weaknesses of our hearts, minds, and bodies. Sometimes listening with our whole selves means we are distracted, closed off, or for some other reason not able to listen with an ear of compassion or selfless care. And that's okay too, because we are not perfect. Our imperfection challenges us to be more intentional and present and committed in our listening, but also to be gentle with ourselves.

> Describe an experience in which you listened to yourself well.
>
> What did it feel like?

Take a moment today to ask St. Benedict to help you to listen with the ear of your heart.

Hospitality

Day 1

All guests . . . are to be welcomed as Christ.

—Rule of Benedict 53.1

Typically we think of hospitality as something offered to another person, like a casserole to a friend who just had a baby, or banana bread to a new neighbor. Benedict invites us to broaden the receiver of our hospitality. We are invited to receive all people, creatures, ideas, experiences, events, words, and spaces as Christ. When I receive the food I eat or the trails I walk on as Christ, it pulls me to care for the land in ways that honor the divinity of all of creation. When I receive a person who grates on my nerves as Christ, it reminds me that he or she too is created in the loving image of God. When I receive an idea that seems egregious to me as Christ, it encourages me to expand my understanding of God's presence and movement in the world.

But how do I receive people who open fire at schools or commit sexual abuse as Christ? I want to engage these people with compassion, thoughtfulness, and openness to God's healing love, but my anger, confusion, and defeat are powerful. Sometimes I am opened by the compassion of a victim closer to the pain than me; other times I need to hand it all over to Christ and pray that one day the healing will work itself open in my heart.

What does it mean to you to "receive as Christ"?

Whom/what is it easy/difficult for you to receive as Christ? Explain.

Take a moment today to receive Christ's never-ending love.

Hospitality

Day 2

[The porter] provides a prompt answer with the warmth of love.

—Rule of Benedict 66.4

The porter is the monastery doorman. Anyone who came to visit a monastery at the time of Benedict met the porter first. Benedict clearly instructs that the porter is to be a "sensible person" who can take a message, deliver a reply, and not wander off—in general, they were to be people of focused presence.

Few of us have doormen, but similar instructions can be applied to how we greet people on a daily basis. I often hear people lament the casual "walk-by" greeting. "Did they really want to hear about my day?" "They didn't even stop walking to listen to my response."

A member of a support group I attend recently commented that our group is one of the only places in his life where he feels safe to say how he truly feels. "I know when someone here asks, 'how are you doing?' they really care to know the answer." Other members of the group chimed agreement. In homes where feelings aren't welcomed, in work spaces where kind conversation isn't efficient, and on streets where speed walking and anonymity are the norm, Benedict's thoughts on porters have a lot to teach us.

Benedict also notes that as soon as anyone knocks on the monastery door, the porter will reply, "Thanks be to God" or "Your blessing, please" (RB 66.3). These seem like goofy greetings to my contemporary ears, but I understand their sense of receiving the guest as a gift. "I'm so glad to see you!" "I've been excited to talk with you all day!" I can imagine Christ waiting at the door to welcome me with this warmth of love.

> With whom is it safe for you to share your feelings and important life experiences?
>
> For whom are you a safe space to share feelings and important life experiences?

Take a moment today to imagine Christ opening the door to you.

Hospitality

Day 3

Care of the sick must rank above and before all else, so that they may truly be served as Christ.

—Rule of Benedict 36.1

I think mothers of young children know something unique about the hospitality of offering their bodies to another person. One friend with a nursing eighteen-month-old came home after an abnormally long day away from her child. Dad was supervising a calm bath time and when Mom walked into the room, the toddler stood up in the bath, dripping wet, extended her arms, and said, "Milk."

Another friend has a two-year-old and is pregnant with her second son. While my friend's body is being transformed by the baby growing inside of her, she rises at 5:15 a.m. because the two-year-old rises then; she chases him around the house and yard to make sure he doesn't eat something he shouldn't, and she uses the restroom, eats lunch, takes a shower, and gets dressed around his nap time, eating needs, and playing.

These women offer their bodies as food for their children, and give up some of their bodily comforts for the sake of their children's well-being. While Benedict may not have written specifically about nursing mothers in the Rule, he was always attentive to people with needs and vulnerabilities.

Describe an experience of your body being a vessel of giving or receiving hospitality.

What did it feel like?

Take a moment today to give thanks for your body, its strengths and its needs.

Community for Ordinary People

Day 1

It was distributed to each as any had need.

—Acts 4:35; see Rule of Benedict 34

I'm so thankful that over and over again St. Benedict made space for human weakness. If the work is strenuous, give the community more food. If the sunlight is fading, shorten the Divine Office. If the weather is cold, hand out more blankets. I would like to think that Benedict's community had a smooth and respectful process for gleaning this wisdom for allowances, but in reality there was probably just as much conflict, arguing, and politicking as our own communities experience when making decisions together.

Maybe the point is not to strive to make decisions without conflict, but to find some way to make decisions together. Tempers will flare. Hurtful things will be said. Sides will be taken. But come together again, weaknesses and all, and admit that we cannot do it alone.

How do you respond when people don't meet your expectations, need your help, or aren't strong?

How do you feel when you need to ask for help?

Take a moment today to remember that just like you, a member of your community is trying to avoid suffering in his or her life.

Community for Ordinary People

Day 2

Love the Lord your God with all your heart, and with all your soul, and with all your mind.

—Matthew 22:37

One day a roommate of mine, a young woman who claims not to be "athletically inclined," came into the kitchen and announced she found a "Couch to 5K" training program. She had never run before but was committed to trying. Several months later I went to her first race and watched my friend run through the streets of the neighborhood with hundreds of others. It was hard work but she did it.

The next year my friend got more ambitious and signed up for a 10K. This time a group of friends gathered to cheer her on. She was great! Afterward, she said it felt wonderful to feel like she and her body could work together to achieve something. The 10K race included half and full marathon runners as well and we stayed to be part of the excitement of watching them finish. As I shouted support and shook a tambourine I'd brought, I watched runners of all shapes and sizes and ages run the final one-eighth of a mile to the finish line. Some participants wore T-shirts declaring their motivations for running, like "In memory of Bob" and "Running to Cure Breast Cancer." Some ran with their friends and family members, others ran along. But the crowd cheered them all on, strangers shouting support and encouragement to other strangers. I was particularly touched to watch one man, wearing brightly striped knee-high socks and a red bandana, run back and forth to help runners in the last few hundred meters before the finish line. They had looks of exhaustion and doubt on their faces, but he told them they could do it . . . and they did.

What do you like about yourself?

When is it challenging for you to follow Jesus' mandate to love yourself?

Take a moment today to name an achievement that you are proud of.

Community for Ordinary People

Day 3

God lives for giving.

—Kevin Seasoltz, OSB

One of my assignments as a student teacher was teaching three sections of Old Testament classes to high school sophomores. Before I took over, my mentor teacher did an introductory lesson on the people we would meet throughout the semester. He talked about Adam and Eve, Noah, Abraham and Sarah, and the rest of the cast as members of a relay team of our faith. The grace of a relay team is that each person carries the baton for a distance, offering his or her contribution, and then passes it on to someone else who is working toward the same goal. Seeking God is the goal of the relay team of our faith.

In chapter 73 of the Rule, Benedict humbly names his Rule as another beginning place for people on the journey to God. The Rule is not the only member of the relay team, but an open door to the Bible, mothers and fathers of the church, other rules for life, other spiritual teachings, and the influences of our own lives.

I'm going to the wake of a member of my relay team tonight: a graduate school professor and monk of Saint John's Abbey. Father Kevin was a brilliant liturgical theologian and editor and taught me courses on sacraments and worship and Eucharist. While Fr. Kevin was a challenging grader and his lectures left our wrists sore from taking so many notes, he was beloved and there was an unofficial fan club. Many key phrases from Fr. Kevin's lectures still sound in my head; one that I hear often is "God lives for giving." All of life is a gift from God: unconditional love, with no strings attached. May we all humbly receive the gifts, and pass them on to future members of the relay team.

Describe a member of the relay team of your faith.

How has that person shaped your way of being in relationships?

Take a moment today to receive all that God wants to give you.

Awareness of God

Day 1

We believe that the divine presence is everywhere.

—Rule of Benedict 19.1

I have a dear friend who loves to have a visual sense of where her loved ones spend their days. For instance, when she comes to visit me, she wants to see me in my space, my apartment, the garden, the monastery—wherever I spend time and with whom I spend time, she wants the visual and firsthand experience. It's a gift to me to take her around and introduce her to people because she is making a web of my life, and she delights in doing it! From my perspective, she is recognizing God in my daily spaces. On any given day I can get in autopilot mode and treat myself, and the people and places around me, as ordinary and mundane. The rhythms and rituals of our lives might not be flashy or glamorous, but they are sacred. With my friend, I see the places I pass every day with new eyes.

"Yes, it's an easy and refreshing walk from the garden, to the library, to the monastery and then home." "Yes, there are beautiful big trees on that side of campus and the flowers are lovely." "Yes, it's a block to the local food co-op if we need an ingredient for supper." Truly God is present in the people and places I see every day, and in the love of a friend who walks into the intimacy of daily life.

How is your response to life experiences affected when you recognize God in them?

Describe a moment of intimacy with a friend, family member, coworker, or stranger in daily life.

Take a moment today to notice God's presence in an everyday experience of your life.

Awareness of God

Day 2

We believe that the divine presence is everywhere.

—Rule of Benedict 19.1

I was playing hide-and-seek with some young friends of mine, and it was my turn to seek. I covered my eyes and counted, and the little ones ran off to various hiding spots around the yard. Just as I counted to ten and started to seek, an adult friend came over and started up a conversation we had begun earlier. We talked and after a few minutes, my young friends started to wonder what was taking me so long and peeked out from their hiding spots. One came up to me, interrupted my conversation, and said, "You are the seeker. Why aren't you seeking us?"

Hide-and-seek is a funny game. It's particularly evident with small children that the ones who are hiding are excitedly waiting to be found. Older children work hard to secure a good hiding spot, and are disappointed when they are exposed, but for small children, the joy of the game is the moment they are found.

I play hide-and-seek in my relationship with God. Sometimes, like the small children, I leave myself wide open to God's pursuit. I recognize that it is by God's grace that joy surrounds me. Other times, like the older children, I intentionally work to create separation. I believe that I can take care of myself, manage the hardships of life, and author my own bliss. But God is always seeking us. Whether we are doing our best to hide, or we are sitting in the middle of the room so as not to be missed, God is constantly seeking greater closeness.

Describe a moment of intimacy with God from the everydayness of your life.

How do these reminders of God's love sustain you?

Take a moment today to play a game with a child.

Awareness of God

Day 3

We believe that the divine presence is everywhere.

—Rule of Benedict 19.1

Our days can easily be filled with tasks to complete, emails to write and respond to, lunches to pack, conflicts to mediate, and laundry to collect, wash, dry, fold, and put away . . . among many other things. But Vietnamese Buddhist monk Thich Nhat Hanh reminds us in *The Miracle of Mindfulness* that a way to practice mindfulness is to "wash the dishes to wash the dishes."[1] He encourages us to live in the moment. As Christians, this means to be present to God's presence in all things; experience God while your hands wash the dinner plates. If we wash the dishes with no other thought but to get on to the next task, we are not living fully.

Sitting still and breathing deeply helps me get back on track when all I can think of is finishing one project to get to the next. When I'm in the garden, rain brings my attention to the present moment. Rain comes and goes without taking notice of my desires, preferences, or goals for the day. But when it rains, I need to stop my work, call the crew inside, and be mindful of the thought that it is raining. Like the rain soaking into the soil, God's presence saturates our lives. When I am being mindful and aware of God's presence, I am often shifted from anxiety to peace, from harshness to humility, and from entitlement to gratitude.

When is it easy/difficult to be in the present moment with God?

What helps/hinders your ability to be aware of God?

Take a moment today to "wash the dishes to wash the dishes."

Note

1. Thich Nhat Hanh, *The Miracle of Mindfulness! A Manual of Meditation*, trans. Mobi Warren (Boston: Beacon Press, 1976), 4.

Moderation

Day 1

All things are to be done with moderation.

—Rule of Benedict 48.9

A friend and I were visiting after hearing a lecture on "Social Movements and Catholic Social Teaching." My friend reflected that Christians understand what it means to be Christian by their context. After hearing about Catholic labor unions around the world, he noted that Christians who struggle to feed their families and have to unite to advocate for changes in their government believe that's what Christians do to live their faith.

My friend then asked, "How does a Christian understand his faith if he grows up in an affluent neighborhood? How is the Gospel preached there?" Douglas Hicks, provost and dean of the faculty at Colgate University and theologian/economist, notes in *On Our Way: Christian Practices for Living a Whole Life* that Jesus teaches, "'One's life does not consist in the abundance of possessions,' (Luke 12:15). Instead, true abundance has to do with being 'rich toward God' (Luke 12:21)."[1] Being "rich toward

God" is not about climbing the corporate ladder and amassing wealth for the sake of doing so. Saint Benedict insisted on a pattern of life that engaged the body, mind, and spirit of people and validated our material experience.

What does it mean to be "rich toward God"? If I am rich toward my sister, I make visiting her a priority, I listen carefully when we talk on the phone, I appreciate who she is, and I share important parts of my life with her. I think that being "rich toward God" asks us to extend that generosity, intentionality, and vulnerability to the world, especially the poorest and most vulnerable around us. Over and over again Jesus calls people to share their material goods with the community around them and focus their lives on God.

What in your life seems abundant right now? (Examples: time, skills, physical strength, outlook on life, prayer, relationships.)

How do you share that abundance?

Where in your life do you practice moderation so that others may have abundance?

Take a moment today to reflect on how you are "rich toward God."

Note

1. Douglas Hicks, "Making a Good Living," in *On Our Way: Christian Practices for Living a Whole Life*, ed. Dorothy C. Bass and Susan R. Briehl (Nashville: Upper Room Books, 2010), 123.

Moderation

Day 2

All things are to be done with moderation.

—Rule of Benedict 48.9

The student gardeners and I recently read chapter 9 from the Rule of Benedict on "The Number of Psalms at the Night Office." Several students come from religious traditions that are less "structured" or liturgical, so the chapter seemed very precise and prescribed to them—rightfully so. Benedict, based on his wisdom, the wisdom of the Scriptures, and the collective wisdom of other spiritual writers, prescribed certain psalms at certain times of day, certain hours at which to pray, certain numbers of hours at which to read, and certain numbers of hours at which to work.

Some people live by their lists and love their lives organized and planned out. Others prefer less structure and choose to let the day unfold however it will. But I imagine that both types appreciate the need to prioritize and make time for what is important to them. Benedict is emphasizing a need for prayer, study, and manual work. There is time in every day for all three, and all three are a way toward God.

Moderation in this sense could refer to balance. What would life be like without one of these three? For myself, I feel off-kilter, lethargic, and disconnected if I work or sit too much, skip prayer, or go too long between visits with family or friends. Moderation isn't just about managing time, but keeping our ultimate values in balance. Benedict's way of life is ultimately about integration for the sake of moving toward God together.

When do you feel most alive as a whole person?

If you were to map out your day or week, what gets most of your attention? How do you feel about that?

Take a moment today to do something life-giving that you've been putting off for another day.

Moderation

Day 3

All things are to be done with moderation.

—Rule of Benedict 48.9

During the garden season I am on my feet for eight hours every day. And I am almost constantly moving—carrying supplies from the barn to the garden, hauling vegetables to be washed and stored in the refrigerators, and walking up and down rows weeding, among so many other things. I have come to accept that I need two fried-egg sandwiches for breakfast to make it through the morning's work; nothing else seems to tide me over. How do we relate to food? How much food, and what kinds "should" we eat? People talk about "guilty pleasures" and berate themselves that "I shouldn't have eaten that" while moaning and rubbing their full tummies.

For Benedict, food is never a penance. In chapter 39 of the Rule on "The Proper Amount of Food," his approach is about generosity, not asceticism. There are options at the dinner table; in case someone doesn't like one dish, he or she can choose the other. And Benedict even goes on to make exceptions for more food when the community's physical labor is heavier. When it comes to food, Benedict says nothing of diets, counting calories, skipping desserts, or guilt or shame of any sort. Food is meant to nourish us and sustain us in our work, prayer, and recreation. Moderation is comfortably eating my two fried-egg sandwiches.

Who in your life models a relationship with food that is based on moderation?

How can you integrate Benedict's teachings on food in your life?

Take a moment today to listen to your body's needs for sustenance.

Stability

Day 1

To stand firm in one's promises.

Benedictines take a vow of stability, and part of that stability is to a physical space. It asserts that God is present in every physical place and, therefore, there is no reason to run around trying to find God someplace else. I asked a sister how she feels about this vow and she responded, "I love knowing this place so intimately. I have favorite curves in the paths through the woods. I look forward to seeing the changing seasons' impact on our prairie. I like visiting other places, but this is my home and God welcomes me back every day."

Esther de Waal, a Benedictine oblate and spiritual writer, astutely points out that this monastic promise of stability pulls against our gut response to run away. When I think of running away, it is because I either feel like a failure or feel unlovable. I think that running away will protect me from hurt that is coming from other people or situations, but really the hurt is coming from inside of me. While it may look like I am running away from others, I am running away from myself and my own ability to gently start anew.

A vow of stability pushes me to stay put, stay with a project, stay at my work, and stay with my prayer when I'd rather run away. Stability, along with the other Benedictine vows of fidelity to a monastic life and obedience, pushes me to listen to myself and to a community that is committed to receiving and giving God's transforming love on a daily basis.

> When are you tempted to run away?
>
> What are you hoping to find someplace else?

Take a moment today to welcome the changing you.

Stability

Day 2

To stand firm in one's promises.

Several years ago I left a full-time job because I felt called into "open space." I didn't have another job I was going to, and I didn't know what was waiting for me in the "open space." A few months into the transition, I was at a gathering at a friend's house where I was meeting some people for the first time. One woman asked me two questions: where did I live, and what was my work? I didn't have an answer for either question and the woman quickly found a way to talk with someone else.

I was hurt and confused by the woman's response, and over time realized that I needed, as Esther de Waal writes, to "find [my] stability in God."[1] Up to that point my stability had been rooted in professional skills, relationships, roles I filled, and responsibilities I had. I needed to prune some of those things back, not because they were bad, but because I needed to make open space for stability in God and myself to grow. It's been a process of coming home to myself, and knowing myself more deeply as I shift from external to internal validation.

In some ways the "open space" was an invitation to instability. In the early stages of the transition time I faced the growthful vulnerability of not being able to call myself a chaplain or campus minister anymore. There were things I liked and disliked about claiming those titles, and instability pushed me to be unattached to all of it. The stability that continues to make a home in me is comfortable with the fluidity of who I am, the roles I have, the responsibilities I take on, and the passions that open me to new opportunities for life. I feel more rooted in God.

What does stability enable you to do or be?

What possibilities does instability offer you?

What does it mean to you to be stable in yourself?

What are your sources of stability?

Take a moment today to welcome instability.

Note

1. Esther de Waal, *Seeking God: The Way of St. Benedict*, 2nd ed. (Collegeville, MN: Liturgical Press, 2001), 56.

Stability

Day 3

To stand firm in one's promises.

At the Common Ground Garden, when the planting is just about complete and the snap peas are about four inches tall, we move into weeding and trellising season. Pea trellises go up first, followed by tomato cages, and lastly cucumber fences. Delicate tendrils on the pea and cucumber plants itch to grab onto and climb up the supports. Tomato plants don't climb by nature, but cages distribute the weight of the fruit, allow air to move through the patch, which diminishes the spread of disease, and of course make picking the produce easier on the gardeners' backs.

In chapter 7 of the Rule, Benedict uses Jacob's ladder (Gen 28:12) as an image of spiritual progress. This ladder and the Rule itself are like garden trellises in that they provide support for people to stand firm in their promises, and enough room for the uniqueness of individual experience, creative expression, and the breath of the Holy Spirit. As Mary Reuter, OSB, writes in

Running with Expanding Heart: Meeting God in Everyday Life, stability is alive and fluid and relaxed and flexible.[1] Sometimes we have difficult choices to make in life: to take a specific job, to marry, or to buy a house in a certain neighborhood. While these choices and the decisions that follow can feel limiting, Benedict's use of the ladder in the Rule encourages us to stand firmly in our values and choices, and receive our stability as a support for new growth.

> Who or what are trellises in your life?
>
> Describe an experience of standing firmly in your convictions while being open to new possibilities.

Take a moment today to stand still, aware of the ground beneath you and possibilities that surround you.

Note

1. Mary Reuter, OSB, *Running with Expanding Heart: Meeting God in Everyday Life* (Collegeville, MN: Liturgical Press, 2010).

Peace

Day 1

No one has the authority to excommunicate or strike any [member of the community] unless . . . given this power by the abbot [or prioress].

—Rule of Benedict 70.2

While Benedict wrote at a time when corporal punishment was normal and commonplace, he did not allow it. Chapter 70 is about more than throwing a few punches, although I believe Benedict would not have condoned that behavior either. Chapter 70 says, "the end does not justify the means." So, "What am I supposed to do instead?" Benedict responds in the next chapter, "good zeal." And what is this "good zeal"? Preferring nothing to Christ's love. Joan Chittister summarizes the two chapters: Benedictine spirituality is not about intimidation and brutality, but personal commitment and community support.[1]

Generally I consider myself a pretty peaceful person. I don't often feel a spirited drive for revenge, and I have to get fairly worked up to want to destroy something—when I do, smashing plates for a mosaic or a speedy bike ride usually calms me down. But what Benedict would call "bitter zeal" is an all-too-regular companion in my life. When I embrace "bitter zeal," I highlight the self-absorbed actions of people around me, call out the mistakes I see in others and name them as failures, and chastise the closed-minded actions of so-called faithful people. Yuck, that's nasty stuff. When I embrace good zeal, on the other hand, I compassionately learn about the lives of my neighbors, I am called to love God more deeply every day, and I am pushed to believe that people are doing the best they can in life.

Describe a person or group who models good zeal.

What prevents you from living good zeal more regularly?

Take a moment today to invite peace into your life.

Note

1. Joan Chittister, *The Rule of Benedict: Insights for the Ages* (New York: Crossroad, 1992), 175.

Peace

Day 2

Pray for your enemies out of love for Christ. If you have a dispute with someone, make peace with him [or her] before the sun goes down.

—Rule of Benedict 4.72-73

Afriend of mine has a bumper sticker on her car that says "peace" in English, Arabic, and Hebrew. One day, as she was getting out of her car in a parking lot, a woman wearing a head scarf approached her. Pointing at the sticker, the woman said, "That's my language!" She seemed genuinely grateful, and went on to say how much it meant to see Arabic connected with the concept of peace. My friend asked why, and the woman told of the discrimination she and her family often faced. Muslim immigrants from the Middle East, she and her husband and two kids had lived in the US for years; he was an engineer and she was a businesswoman. They lived a typical, urban American life, but they were not treated like typical Americans. She talked about being harassed on the street, being stared at in stores, being called names; once, a man threw hot coffee on her through her open car window. She didn't seem angry as she retold these stories, just sad. She said she just wanted her children to grow up in a place where they didn't experience hate.

I've always admired my friend's bumper sticker. To me, it encourages that peace is not just a nice thing I should spread among people who speak my language. The limits of peace should expand across cultures, languages, faith traditions, and continents, let alone railroad tracks, backyards, and dinner tables. "Peace, Salaam, Shalom" also reminds me that Americans, English speakers, Christians (or any other groups that we belong to) do not have a monopoly on peace. We all desire peace. Mothers and fathers across the world desire opportunities for their children to succeed. Factory workers and farmers desire dignifying work, just payment, and safe working conditions. And we all desire secure and calm places to rest our tired bodies at the end of our work and play, so we can rise refreshed and ready for a new day.

Who is it easy/difficult for you to extend peace to?

How do you define peace and living a peaceful life?

Take a moment today to sing a song about peace (for example, "Let There Be Peace on Earth," "Make Me a Channel of Your Peace," or "Peace Is Flowing Like a River").

Peace

Day 3

Pray for your enemies out of love for Christ. If you have a dispute with someone, make peace with him [or her] before the sun goes down.

—Rule of Benedict 4.72-73

As the parents of a good friend of mine celebrated forty years of marriage, they shared a maxim that they've tried to live by: do not go to bed angry. In Matthew's gospel Jesus tells the disciples, "when you are offering your gift at the altar, if you remember that your brother or sister has something against you, leave your gift there before the altar and go; first be reconciled to your brother or sister, and then come and offer your gift" (Matt 5:23-24). As I think of my friend's parents—and all couples trying to live this out—I imagine gentle waves softening battered egos as both people recognize that their love for each other is more important than the source of their argument.

Sometimes peace feels like an intangible thing that is described by what it is not. I want peace and not war. I want peace and not anxiety. I want peace and not violence. The prophet Isaiah says, "The wolf shall live with the lamb, / the leopard shall lie down with the kid . . . The nursing child shall play over the hole of the asp . . . They will not hurt or destroy / on all my holy mountain; / for the earth will be full of the knowledge of the LORD / as the waters cover the sea" (Isa 11:6, 8-9). All of this suggests that peace is a response of love in the face of conflict. The love of God must be pretty strong to be able to wash over some of the hurts or harm that come our way.

God always takes the first step toward us. Any compassion, generosity, kindness, thoughtfulness, or healing that I offer to myself, the earth, or others is first gifted to me. God is the source, so that we may not go to bed angry.

What does peace initiated by God look like?

Who/what are a "wolf" and a "lamb" in your life that will live together in peace?

Take a moment today to receive God's peace.